The Snow

Phyllis Sunday

Illustrated by Md. Hemayet Uddin

ISBN-13: 978-1519505590
ISBN-10: 1519505590

Illustrated by
Md. Hemayet Uddin

Interior Design by
Woven Red Author Services

*Dedicated to
my nieces and nephews*

Phyllis Sunday has spent over a decade working with children of all age groups.

Books by the author are:
Book of Poems
You Promised
The Infant
Thank You, Lord
The Beggar

The snow
is like
white rain

pouring down from the heavens.

illuminating the atmosphere
with its natural beauty.

It dresses the meadows

and evergreens,

and coats the houses with its flair.

The snowfall could be
light or heavy,

icy or flaky.

The fresh snow can be gleaming and glistening, fulgent and effulgent,

glowing and glinting,
bright and dazzling,
or shiny and sparkling.

The old, dirty snow can be
glassy and greasy like a skating ring,
satiny and silky,

sleek and slippery,
unsteady and unstable,
soapy and sticky,
or wet and waxy.

Winter is never winter
without snowfall.
The fresh snowfall—
the darling of winter—

makes such a stunning sight!
Oh, how I long for
the fresh snowfall!

www.ingramcontent.com/pod-product-compliance
Lightning Source LLC
Chambersburg PA
CBHW060824290526
45792CB00005BB/1781